ISBN-13: 978-0692279984

ISBN-10: 0692279989

Copyright © 2014 by Author LaTersa Blakely. The book author retains sole copyright to her contributions to this book.

Disclaimer: LaTersa Blakely does not assume and hereby disclaims any liability to any part for any loss or damage by errors or omissions in this publication, whether such errors or omissions result from negligence, accident or any other cause. To ensure complete accuracy, it is always best to call and confirm that the information is still up-to-date.

This book cannot be duplicated in any form whatsoever without written permission from the author.

LaTersa Blakely Enterprises, Inc.: http://www.latersablakely.com

Facebook: http://www.facebook.com/theoriginalentrepreneur

Twitter: http://www.twitter.com/momswearinghats

Blog: http://www.mommymavensrock.com

Acknowledgments

I want to thank God for allowing me this opportunity and the mind to share the life lessons and knowledge I have learned with other moms and mom entrepreneurs. I would like to thank my husband for believing in my dream since day one and giving me the seed money to start my entrepreneurial journey; and last but not least, my two amazing and darling little ones, Ishmael and Sarah. Mommy loves you very much.

Additionally, I want to thank all the wonderful moms, moms-to-be and awesome mom entrepreneurs, because truly, you are the original entrepreneurs and Proverbs 31 women. I also want to thank my fans and followers who have supported me throughout the years and have trusted me to bring you nothing but the best. I'm forever grateful.

Credits

Author: LaTersa D. Blakely

Editor: brownchickediting.com

Cover: http://robyngaskinssmith.com/

Dedication

I dedicate this book to all the amazing moms, moms-to-be, mompreneurs – aspiring and experienced. All things are possible to those who believe in God. The Lord said your gifts and talents will make room for you; so now, it's time for you to get creative, reach within your soul, and pull out all God has equipped you with.

Content

The Ideal~ Introduction	11
Chapter One~ Proverbs 31 Woman	15
Chapter Two~ How to Create Money	20
Chapter Three~ How to Manage Money	26
Chapter Four~ How to Balance Work & Family	31
Chapter Five~ How to Increase Your Time Management Skills	36
Chapter Six~ How to Take Care of Yourself	40
Chapter Seven~ A New Season of New Opportunities	42
Chapter Eight~ Create an Environment That's Functional	48
Chapter Nine~ A Glimpse into LaTersa's Life	52
Chapter Ten~ How to Balance Life as a Single Married Woman	60
Quotes For Moms	64
Book Recommendations	66
Author	67
Mommy's Journal	72

The Ideal:

When my kids were very young, and I worked outside the home, I needed day care for two children who were both in diapers. It was very clear to me that I was working just to pay childcare, so I became a little frustrated and would complain every time pay day came. I would have to literally give almost my complete check – all but $20 – to the daycare facility. I was thinking, *I'm in the wrong profession, because here I am, working eight to five every day, 40 hours a week, and every two weeks, I have to turn over my entire check.* Something had to change. Something was completely wrong, because this was not what life was supposed to be.

After a year of doing that, my husband and I decided it was best that I come home, at least until the kids were older and became school-aged. And that's when I began my entrepreneurial journey. Did I have a plan B? No, I didn't, and I wouldn't recommend not having one to anybody. But I put my two weeks' notice in and set out on my journey as a stay-at-home mom. Since I love crafts, and I loved creating my diaper cakes, I figured why not turn this into a business? I can be my own boss, make my own money and not have to clock in at a nine-to-five.

Well, reality set in, and I was going insane, pulling my hair out the first few months. I was like, *What the heck have I just done?* Not only did I not know what to do with my business, I was also trying to make sure the house was clean and that the kids were okay, while running behind them every day. Although I was burned out, I knew I wanted to start my business. I just didn't know how to juggle that with being a good wife, mom, and making sure the house was neat. So, I had to learn how to be a wife and mother.

One thing people don't understand is that getting married doesn't make you a wife. You have to ask God to help you become one because things will be different. It's no longer about just you; it's about you, your husband, and your kids. If you want to be selfish, being a wife is not for you.

I also had to learn how to run a business. The entrepreneurial bug bit me in childhood. Whether I was typing papers and reports, baking cakes for neighbors or classmates or designing gift baskets and sewing pillows, I would do different things to earn extra money. So, I decided to come home to start a business and be with my children because that's what I really wanted to do. I'd always wanted to be a mom, and staying at home would allow me to do so I wanted to be there to see their first steps and create memories with them so when they become adults, they'll have something to look back on. Being a stay-at-home mom and entrepreneur gives me the opportunity to do that. If I want to participate in their field trips, I can do that since my schedule is flexible as opposed to when I worked a nine-to-five. If one of my kids got sick, I had to check with my boss to get off work. In fact, at my last job, I was written up a lot; I had to take off because my kids were sick so much. That's where I drew the line: I decided I would no longer put a nine-to-five job before my kids.

There was one incident in particular that made my decision to leave easier: when my son had a really bad nose bleed. I spoke with my supervisor and told her I had to go, and she told me that I'd have to decide if I wanted to be a mom or continue working there. I'd even let her know during my interview that if something happened to Ishmael or Sarah, then I'd have to go. I would not choose my job over my children.

Being that my husband was the breadwinner, he couldn't take off much so I had to. Yes, I was written up, but it was well worth it because I was able to take my son to the emergency room to get his nose bleed under control and make sure nothing else was going on.

That, in a nutshell, is how I became a stay-at-home mom and entrepreneur. I know so many of you are looking for a way you can come home and be with your children. You're tired of being told you have to choose between your job and your kids, and if your kids get sick, you have to call a family member to take care of them when really, that's your responsibility. But because you need the money, you can't afford to take off. That was the inspiration behind this book, Mom the original entrepreneur. No matter what's going on, you choosing your household is the best way to go. This is a guide to help you figure out what you can do at home to earn profit and help your husband with the household, bills, and be able to take care of your family. I want you to sit back, get a glass of wine (or drink of your choice), relax, and enjoy the rest of this book.

Chapter 1: Proverbs 31 Woman

What is a Proverb 31 Woman? I'm going to give you my definition before I tell you exactly what the Bible says about her. She is a bad – shut your mouth. She has it going on in every way possible. From just reading about her, I know she is a woman who is-confident and a woman who knows she is enough.

    I feel that each and every one of you is a Proverbs 31 woman, but you've got to let her out. She's suffocating inside of you and wants to come out. Read what God says a Proverbs 31 woman is:

Who can find a virtuous woman? for her price is far above rubies. The heart of her husband does safely trust in her, so that he shall have no lack of gain. She will do him good and not evil all the days of her life. She seeks wool, and flax, and works willingly with her hands. She is like the merchants' ships; she brings her food from afar. She rises also while it is yet night, and gives food to her household, and a portion to her maidservants.

Proverbs 31:10-15 KJV

This tells us that she takes care of her home. She is not a lazy woman; she's always looking for work. She's busy creating things with her hands to make money. She cares for her kids and supports her husband. She also "…rises while it is still night." Even when her family is sleeping, she's up, preparing food and getting her home ready.

She considers a field, and buys it: with the fruit of her hands she plants a vineyard.

Proverbs 31:16

A Proverbs 31 woman goes out, finds work, plants her seeds and watches them grow.

She girds her loins with strength, and strengthens her arms. She perceives that her merchandise is good: her lamp goes not out by night.

Proverbs 31:17-18 KJV

Not only does she create valuable things for her family, she also sells them, making a profit to support her husband. Her lamp never goes out at night, which means she's burning the midnight oil.

She lays her hands to the distaff, and her hands hold the spindle. She stretches out her hand to the poor; yea, she reaches forth her hands to the needy. She is not afraid of the snow for her household: for all her household are clothed with scarlet. She makes herself coverings of tapestry; her clothing is fine linen and purple.

Proverbs 31:19-22 KJV

She sews clothes for her family. She makes linen for the beds in her home. She is not a lazy woman; she is the original entrepreneur. And that's what you are! As women, we're born nurturers. We are caregivers at heart. We take care of family, our children and husbands.

Her husband is known in the gates, when he sits among the elders of the land. She makes fine linen, and sells it; and delivers sashes unto the merchants. Strength and honor are her clothing; and she shall rejoice in time to come. She opens her mouth with wisdom; and on her tongue is the law of kindness.

Proverbs 31:23-26 KJV

This woman is not some loose woman; she carefully monitors what comes out of her mouth. Remember, the power of life and death is in the tongue.

She looks well to the ways of her household, and eats not the bread of idleness.

Proverbs 31:27 KJV

The Proverbs 31 woman stays busy and focuses on building up her own household, so she doesn't have time to covet what others have. She's content and happy with what she has.

Her children arise up, and call her blessed; her husband also, and he praises her. Many daughters have done virtuously, but you excel them all. Charm is deceitful, and beauty is vain: but a woman that fears the LORD, she shall be praised. Give her of the fruit of her hands; and let her own works praise her in the gates.

Proverbs 31: 28-31 KJV

This is a woman of worth. She knows who she is and is confident. And because she pleases God, she is blessed.

This woman takes care of her household. She looks for things to create to earn a profit. She cares for her children and husband and maintains a clean home. You, too, are a Proverbs 31 woman, a virtuous woman!

Chapter 2: How to Create Money

Creating money is something we all want to do; that's the ultimate goal. As the original entrepreneurs, we want to be home with our families and also be able to contribute financially, right? This chapter is all about ways you can create money while being home with your children as a stay-at-home mom.

Craft Business

If you're a crafty woman who loves to sew, create gift baskets, pillows, or throws, you can establish a craft business. You can sell your crafts on websites like bonanza.com, etsy.com, or ebay.com. Before you begin selling, do your research. You don't want to start a business just because it's something you're passionate about. Be sure there's a demand for it. You can have the greatest idea, but if nobody wants it, then you'll just have an expensive hobby. Buying material can get costly, especially if nobody's purchasing your products; you don't want to waste your money or time.

In-Home Childcare Service

If you like children, you may consider starting a babysitting business. You can care for three to five kids in your home each day and charge the going rate. Do some research to find out the average rate.

Writing or Editing Services

Love to write? That's a great way to earn extra money at home. You can find freelance jobs on websites like elance.com or odesk.com. Additionally, you can write articles for magazines or blogs. You can even create an editing company, working on books, research papers, or articles.

Gift Business

A gift business is how I began my entrepreneurial journey. As a crafty mom, I started mine because I loved creating gift baskets. I took it a step further with the diaper cake, diapers formed in the shape of a cake. You can list your items on websites like easy.com, bonanza.com, and ebay.com, which are free to use. You can also start a YouTube channel, showing others how to design gifts and direct people to your website.

I was known as the rock star mom entrepreneur since everybody knew me for my diaper cakes. People began to know, like, and trust me; and that's important when starting a home-based business. You must to get to know your audience, let them get to know you, then form a relationship where they trust you. One way to build great relationships is to offer something of value at no cost such as a white paper or ebook (we'll talk more about that later). Building relationships is key when it comes to being a successful entrepreneur and selling your products and services.

Candle/Soap Business

If you enjoy making candles or soaps, you can sell them online or at local events. If you're not interested in selling them, you can teach people how to make them through workshops or online classes.

Network Marketing Company

I supplement my income through network marketing. I currently work with DS Domination at www.workwithlatersa.com. Through this company, I'm empowering other moms, just like you, to add to their incomes by selling on eBay and drop shipping from Amazon.

Garage Sales

If you need extra money to build your home-based business or for your household, have a garage sale.

Cleaning Service Business

Many moms love to clean, and if you're one of them, consider starting your own cleaning service. You can advertise on websites like Craigslist or in your local newspaper. You can also purchase business cards from vistaprint.com for as little as $10 to promote your service

Cookbook (Ebook)

Love to cook? Create a cookbook! Take your top 10 recipes, and write an ebook. To create one, type your recipes in a document, save it as a PDF, and there's your cookbook. On websites like fiverr.com (where people offer services for just $5), you can hire someone to design your ebook cover, then upload it to a website like payhip.com to sell it.

Photography

If you enjoy taking pictures, a photography business may be the way to go. To earn money, you might decide to specialize in a certain area such as weddings, commercial photography or events. Place an ad on your local Craigslist board or newspaper to promote your services.

Run Errands For Other Stay-at-home Moms or the Elderly

You can do things like take people to their doctor's appointments, pick up dry cleaning, go grocery shopping, pay their bills, or pick up their prescriptions.

Fitness Coach

If you are a fitness guru and love being healthy, create a workout program via YouTube, or develop private classes where attendees pay a monthly fee for workout regimens. Live classes can be held via skype.com or Google hangout. If you want to add extra income in the fitness area, consider joining Herbal life and becoming a distributor or recommending it to your clients. I currently use the products to help me watch my weight. I'll provide a link later on where you can get more information.

Info-products/Online Classes

This is one of my favorite ways to earn money. I teach people how to make the gifts I used to design and sell. People are always looking for information, so get paid for what you know.

These are just a few ideas for making money from home. Hopefully, one of these ideas gets your juices flowing and on the path to becoming a home-based entrepreneur.

Chapter 3: How to Manage Money

Money is a beautiful thing; don't let anybody tell you it's not. Money allows you to take those lavish family vacations. It allows you to put your kids through school with a college fund, and it allows you to have great, affordable insurance for your family, so money is a good thing. However, you must understand how important it is to manage your finances. If you can't manage $5, how are you going to ask God to bless you with $5,000? You'll just find a way to blow that, too.

Getting Started With Money Management

Now is the time for you to learn how to better manage your money. When you're starting out as a stay-at-home mom and building your home-based business, it's wise to have two separate accounts. Do not mix your business account with your personal one; I've been there, done that, and it doesn't work at all. I know that as a solo entrepreneur, there are great tax write-offs for home-based businesses, but still, you need separate accounts.

The first step in managing and creating your business is to establish yourself as a sole proprietor. Contact your local tax agency, accountant, or your state tax representative for more information. Make sure to get your business license and if required, zoning and seller's permits. In Pittsburgh, for example, you must obtain a business license and a seller's permit. Plus, you want to make sure that you're not violating any zoning permits.

Managing Your Money

Statistics show that 58 percent of Americans do not have retirement plans, and the average household credit card debt is $15,204. These numbers tell us that money, if not handled wisely, can become detrimental to your lifestyle.

Here are a few tips on how you can start managing your money better:

- **Create a budget.** A budget is simply an estimate of your expected income and expenses. You want to have an idea of where your money is going. One way to do this is to track your income and expenses for one month to find out exactly where your money is going; doing this will give you an idea of how to better spend your money and keep more of it.

Take a sheet of paper (or open a document or your computer or tablet), and write down your income for the month. Underneath, write "Expenses." List your rent/mortgage, your household bills (utilities, electric, gas), your grocery expenses, entertainment and personal care (like dining out or getting your hair done), gas for your car, medical expenses, and savings. Also, be realistic; don't say you'll put $500 in your savings account when you can only afford $200. Start with that, and grow from there. You want to be sure to set some money aside for a rainy day because unexpected things *do* occur.

Keeping track of what's going in and coming out will allow you to set your household budget realistically.

- **Look for ways to save.** Instead of going out for dinner every other day, for example, cook at home. Use Redbox instead of buying DVDs, or subscribe to Netflix and cut back on or even cancel your cable. If you have a mortgage, double up on the payment some months if you can.

- **Improve your credit score.** One way you can increase your credit score is by using your debit card to pay your household expenses. Additionally, if you do have credit cards, make sure you're paying your monthly balance on time, and try to pay more than the minimum. It will take you much longer to pay off your credit card if you make only the minimum payment each month.

- **Only spend what you have.** Don't spend what you think you're going to make, especially in business. For instance, don't go out spending money just because you have a *potential* client. Using the money you actually have will keep you from a lot of stress (this includes using your credit card as well: Don't buy things you can't afford to pay off monthly). Keep cash on you; if you can't pay for an item with cash, then more than likely, you don't need it. A good rule of thumb (and something I used to do): If I saw an outfit I felt I really needed, I gave it a week. I'd hide it among the other clothes, then come back in a week. If it was still there, then that meant it was for me. If it wasn't, then I didn't need it.

- **Invest your money wisely.** There are many books on investing out there, whether you're just starting out or are already investing and want to learn more. Also, you can talk to people who are knowledgeable on the subject. Additionally, if your job, or your spouse's job, offers a 401 (k), find out ways you can wisely invest in it.

- **Acquire good insurance.** They say that smart people expect the unexpected and have a plan for what they'll do just in case. You never know when you'll need a nice sum of money for an emergency, so it's wise to have good insurance for your family. If, God forbid, your spouse passes, you want to be sure you have good burial policies; and if there's a fire or theft in your home, homeowners insurance helps.

- **Create an emergency fund.** As I mentioned earlier, you never know what life may bring you. Your spouse may get laid off, and if you're just starting to work from home, things may get tight. Even if you can only put away a couple of hundred dollars per month, do so. Every little bit helps.

- **Form a debt payment plan.** And don't create more debt. There are many online resources that can assist you in getting started with this.

Dr. Maya Angelou said, "When you know better, you do better." Prayerfully, these tools and tips will help you manage your money better and assist you in becoming a great steward over your resources, because God can't bless you with more if you can't handle what he's already given you.

Chapter 4: How to Balance Work and Family

Most, if not all, women crave balance in our work and families. How do we juggle the two? How do we keep everything in tact without losing our minds? How do we maintain our homes, and how do we keep our businesses separate from our families? How do we keep everything in perspective? These questions, and their answers, are what we'll explore in this chapter.

I want to share a few quick tips you can start using today to balance work and family.

- When it comes to business, **determine the amount of time you're going to spend on social media**. As you probably know, social media is the new thing now, and it's essential if you're an entrepreneur. Face-to-face interaction is still great too, but many business relationships are built online so you want to carve out time for it. If you spend all day on social media, you'll look up, and it'll be 3:00 PM and you won't have anything accomplished. My rule of thumb: Automate my posts while checking in every one to two hours. When I check in, I look to see if anybody's commented on anything I've posted because I want to engage with my audience, which is important, particularly when you're building a home-based business.

- **Get your family involved.** Allow your spouse to see what you do, and try to find ways for him to participate if he's interested. This will help him better understand what you do, and when he sees the results from your venture, he'll be more likely to get on board (if he's not already). You can allow your children to do some things in your business as well. My daughter has been creating diaper cakes with me since she was about two. I used to let her play with the old diapers while watching me work, and now she could probably design a diaper cake herself. She also does videos with me, especially when I talk about balancing work, life, and love. You'd be surprised at what a six-year-old can tell you about balance. I allow my son to do some things with me as well. Involve your family when you start your business, and they'll feel like they're a part of the team, and that's what you want because it *is* a team effort. It will take all of you working together for the common good to be successful.

Schedule distinct times for working on your business and hanging out with your family. I suggest setting an alarm for an hour or two to focus on income-producing activities. You could be spending a lot of time being busy but not profiting. That's not a business; that's an expensive hobby. It's nerve-wracking, and you'll really want to pull your hair out then. Carve out time to do the activities that will allow your business to grow.

When you're starting out, it may be wise to hire an assistant to do those things you don't really enjoy doing, like following up with prospective clients. This will take away some of your stress, and you'll be able to focus more on things that generate an income in your business, while allowing your assistant to handle tasks such as calling and following up with clients and answering emails. If you're not sure where to find help, try websites like elance.com, fiverr.com, or odesk.com.

- **Make time to do fun stuff with your kids and spouse.** Family comes first. Don't get so caught up in building your business that you neglect your family. If you do, it will put a strain on your marriage and on your children. They'll feel left out because you're so focused on your business and not spending time with them. You must make time to spend with your family.

My babies were in diapers when I became a stay-at-home mom entrepreneur. So, my schedule went something like this: I got up, cooked breakfast, and washed the dishes. I took the kids to the park in the morning, especially during the summer so they could wear themselves out. Then, we'd come back home, I fixed their lunch, and they took a nap. While they napped, I'd either take a power nap or work on my business. You can always find ways to be as productive as possible. It's just going to take some time and a little trial and error to determine what works for you.

Self-Care Is A Must

Taking care of yourself should be a top priority. If you're not taking care of you, you'll be out of whack. Everything will be unbalanced. When you're not taking care of yourself, you're probably not taking care of your kids properly because you're tired. You're not loving on or caring for your spouse. So, make sure you're taking care of you first (I'll go more into this in a later chapter).

One way you can care for yourself is to manage your time wisely. Get a big calendar, and write down what you need to get done daily. I personally like to do business activities first thing in the morning. Remember, being a stay-at-home mom doesn't mean you have to spend all day cleaning the house, washing dishes, and cooking. Schedule time to do those specific things. If you want your house to look tidy, maybe you can hide those dishes in the dishwasher until you get ready to wash them; at least the sink will be clean. Also, take out the trash because you don't want the house to stink. You could even hire a maid or maid service to come in once a week, every two weeks, or once a month to give your house a big clean.

Another option is to hire a nanny to come in for a couple of hours to watch the kids while you work on your business. Acquiring outside help doesn't make you a bad mom or wife. It just shows that you need assistance, so don't be afraid to ask for it.

If you don't work your business then guess what? You don't get paid. You can't expect to see results if you're not putting in the work and investing in yourself and your business. When starting out, you may not have a lot of money to invest; that means you have to invest time in researching your industry, finding out who your competition is and who is successful in your field.

For more assistance, reach out to someone you admire, who's been where you're trying to go, and ask him or her to be your mentor. Nine times out of 10, you'll get a yes; people are usually willing to help someone who's helping herself. If you're not sure who to contact, you can try places like score.org, which I've used. I reached out when I started my business, and they gave me a lot of tips on business plans. And that's something you want to have in your business. You need something to aim for and some goals. I also suggest setting goals for your family.

When creating your goals, make sure they're realistic and smart. Additionally, don't set goals that will add stress; you'll have enough stress as it is with the many hats you wear. Finally, remember: "A goal without a plan is just a wish."

Chapter Five: How to Increase Your Time Management Skills

If you struggle with time management, perhaps it's time to take a look at a few suggestions. However, the truth is, there are no hard rules for time management. What works for your friends may not work for you, and that's okay. At the beginning of my entrepreneurial journey, managing my time and finding balance was a major problem. But through trial and error, I've found what works for me.

Below I've shared some of my top tips for bettering your time management:

1. Close your door, and turn off the phone. If you need to complete an important task, it's important to avoid unnecessary interruptions. Sitting alone can certainly help you clear your head and get things done. Also, if you're using the Internet, resist the urge to check your social media accounts.

2. Have a home for common items. When you get home, always place items like your keys and wallet in the same place. The next time you go out, you won't have to waste precious time looking for them.

3. Change your behavior. If you've identified a certain behavior that's counterproductive to your time management, take steps to correct it.

For example, if you always take lunch breaks that are too long, set a timer so you can return to your duties on time.

4. Minimize, then organize your documents. A lot of information is digital-only these days, but you don't need to keep every email, file, or document on your computer's desktop. Delete what's unnecessary, organize files in folders, and only keep documents you're actively using at your fingertips.

5. Estimate your time. Whether you're doing a work assignment or something fun, plan in advance how long you think it will take. If you remain aware of the time, you won't lose a few hours without realizing it.

6. Less planning, more action. How often do you find yourself thinking about what you have yet to do? Merely thinking about the future won't get you anywhere. Strive to live in the now, and take action to complete your tasks.

7. Avoid procrastination. This is a difficult one for many people. When you keep putting something off that needs to be accomplished, you tend to spend more time thinking about the fact that you have to do it when you could have used that time to complete the task.

Quit making excuses, and develop the willpower to do the things you're not fond of doing. Once you do it, you'll strengthen your resolve and build momentum.

8. Set goals. Setting goals is an important part of any plan. When you're working, it's far easier to track your progress and complete your task more efficiently if you have a specific goal to achieve.

9. Reward yourself. Treat yourself for a job well done. A reward motivates you to get through the tougher tasks and avoid procrastination.

Remember, it's important to have some fun in life!

10. Take breaks. While it's important to be self-disciplined, you don't want to overdo it and burn out. Mental breaks actually boost your productivity because your mind has a chance to reflect, rejuvenate, and repair itself.

Schedule frequent 10 minute breaks to clear your mind.

Final Advice

The most important thing to remember about time management is to find something that works for *you*. Start by paying attention to your habits and decisions so you can identify when you feel tempted to waste time and procrastinate. If you keep taking steps in the right direction, you'll soon conquer the time wasters that have kept you from success for far too long.

Chapter Six: Take Care of Yourself First

As mothers, we tend to get so caught up in taking care of everyone else that we often forget about self. Well, I'm here to tell you that a hard head makes a very soft behind (as my mama used to say). Your body needs rest and plenty of it. And if you have infants in the house, it's imperative that you get as much rest as possible because you *will* definitely need it.

Physical Health

Get your pelvic examination, and visit your doctors on a regular basis. Most importantly, eat balanced meals daily and drink plenty of water. I sometimes forget to drink mine. Not because I don't like it, but because I'm so busy starting my day, getting things done on my to-do list and taking care of everyone else that I don't even look at a bottle of water. But, I'm working on it, and I now keep a bottle by my bed and on my desk.

Mental Health

When I first got married, I literally acted like I was super woman. I tried so hard to make everything perfect, and if one thing got out of place, I was upset. I wanted my hubby to see that everything was taken care of and that I was in complete control. Well, I soon landed myself a sweet little vacation to the ER (but we'll talk about that in a little while). I want you to understand that it's okay to not have everything in its perfect little place. No, you are not a bad mother or wife if you happen to leave a few loads of laundry undone. There is always tomorrow, so you don't have to try to get everything done in one day.

Chapter Seven: A New Season & Opportunities

It was a bit of a bad first year in business! And it was scary. People don't tell you what you need to know when starting a business. You pretty much only hear about the glamor and glitz, like how much money you'll make as your own boss. Well, I had a wake-up call, and boy, was it an eye opener.

When I first started out, my company was called The LaTersa Diaper Cakes, and I designed gifts such as diaper cakes, towel cakes, gift baskets and more. You name it, I designed it. Being crafty is what's in my heart, and it brings me so much joy! I grew up with my mother and grandmother, and they taught me how to knit, sew and bake.

In 2010, my business was like a roller coaster. I would make money one week, and the next week, there would be nothing; this went on for about a year and a half. I spent a lot of money, but I wasn't making much. I attended every craft show that came to town, set up my cute little booth and put my diaper cakes on display. I did well at some of them, and other times, I wouldn't even break even.

Fast forward to fall 2010: I sat down to do my taxes, and I could have fallen out of my chair when I found that I was $3,000 in the negative. I said to myself, *How in the world did I do that when I didn't even make that kind of money?* I was so frustrated, I had to put my taxes down for a bit. Now, you know you have to give your spouse an explanation when something goes wrong. I dreaded it for a few days, but I finally told him. Let's just say it didn't go too well. From that point on, I knew I had to do something different, so I hired a business coach. And I discovered that I needed to set up my business model another way, or I would be setting myself up for the same results, year after year.

By early 2011, I was determined to do things differently, so I revised my business plan, got some coaching sessions lined up, and I must say, things began to look up. I was generating income in my business, and I didn't have to ask hubby for extra money. But lo and behold, I hit a dry patch again. There I was, enjoying my gifts and favors but no money. I was truly beginning to feel like this entrepreneurship stuff was not working for me, and I even thought about going back to my regular nine-to-five. But I realized I didn't want to be supervised or take orders from anyone again.

While there really is no one way to do this thing called mom entrepreneurship, I have more tips on how I keep everything flowing and making sure my hubby and the little people are happy. When I first started my journey as a mom entrepreneur, I made some not-so-great decisions, and I'm still growing. Below are some mistakes to avoid when starting your business:

1. **Don't quit your regular job without a plan and system in place for your transition.** I got fed up with my supervisor not appreciating my work and effort, so I put in my two weeks' notice. I loved making diaper cakes and gift baskets so much that I figured I could make extra money doing what I love. Well, that backfired because it wasn't what I thought it would be.

2. **No business plan.** I went into this thing blindly with just an idea and a prayer. I didn't think about all the details and things you needed to have in place. I sort of thought I could just be successful. I mean, I have my degrees, and I'm pretty intelligent, right? I made the mistake of trying to get all of my products seen by others before I had a clear plan for marketing them. You need a blueprint so you have a sense of direction. As the saying goes, 'You don't know where you're going if you don't map out your directions.' Even if you don't know exactly how to write a business plan, start by brainstorming and writing down the ideas and goals you want to accomplish in your business. After you do that, find a mentor or an expert in your field who can help you create a business plan. One place to start is www.score.org. Score serves entrepreneurs, locally and nationwide; just go to the web site, type in your location, and choose from mentors in your area. Once you have your

business plan, you'll see an actual strategy and have an idea of where you're going.

3. **No savings.** I didn't have any savings, nor did I have any startup money. Everything was on my husband, and I just knew my business would blow up and be on Oprah's 100. Because I didn't plan or have any funds, I couldn't invest in my business and line things up from the start.

4. **I thought I could do this alone.** Yes, really; I thought, *How bad could this be?* Boy was I in for a rude awakening. I nearly drove myself insane. I was doing everything from cleaning the house to doing the laundry and taking care of the kids and hubby. But I left out one ingredient: myself. I didn't realize it until I landed myself a little trip to the ER, and I was told my thyroid hormones were too low. I had no energy, and I was very weak. While I ended up staying a few days, I'm happy to say I'm much better now.

5. **I told almost everyone my plan.** When you're getting ready to step out on faith and follow your dreams, not everyone will be in agreement with you. I had to learn this the hard way. Those who really know me know that when I have a great idea, and even when the smallest thing happens, I get happy and

excited. So, I talked about my plans of starting my own business and being my own boss to just about anyone who listened. I was so thrilled and overjoyed that I'd finally found my niche, my passion, my dream, and purpose. I was ecstatic that I had taken my desire to make people smile, created gift baskets, and turned it into a business. Unfortunately, I had individuals tell me that my business wouldn't make it and that people wouldn't buy diaper cakes and gift baskets because selling them wasn't a real job. I let all that negative talk go in one ear and out the other. One thing you'll get to know about me is people saying I can't, is my motivation to prove them wrong.

The next time you have a great idea or want to start something new, keep it between you and God and maybe one or two people in your circle. Not everyone will believe in your dreams, but as long as you believe in them and in God, He will bring them to pass.

6. **Don't give up!** I cannot stress this enough! Any time you want something great or are starting something great, you *will* go through obstacles. There have been times when I've felt like giving up, but that little voice inside of me wouldn't let me rest. When these moments happen, you have to rely on your faith in God, and surround yourself with like-minded and positive

people. Your inner circle of friends and family will be there to uplift you when you're feeling down. Keep your eye on the prize, and block out everything that's hindering you from being successful. This may mean you have to let people go, whether they are family members, friends, or co-workers. Whatever you have to do to keep your mind healthy so you can function well, by all means, do it.

I hope this inspires and helps you give your business another chance. If you need assistance or want to check out my business, you can do so by calling me or going to my website, www.mommymavensrock.com, for clarity.

Chapter Eight: Create an Environment That's Functional

When you're a mom entrepreneur, you have to learn how to balance work and family, and this requires having a system. If you don't have some sort of system in place for running your home business and taking care of your family, you will quickly fail or drive yourself crazy. Here is how I function at my best on a daily basis:

1. **I cultivate an attitude of gratitude.** If you start your morning with a grateful state of mind, you set the tone for the remainder of your day. Being grateful also allows you to keep things in perspective.

2. **I make a daily to-do list.** Do you know how many moms wake up every day and just wing it? They don't have anything set for what they intend to achieve for that particular day. I make a to-do list every night before I go to bed; having one helps me stay focused on the most important things I need to get done. I suggest writing your list with three main categories: Personal, Business and Family. Then, put two things in each section you must get done on that given day. You can put more, but have at least two priorities for each one. Don't beat yourself up if you don't get everything

done on your list; as long as you accomplish the main things, celebrate by crossing them off. I promise it will make you feel so amazing.

3. **I keep a positive attitude**. Doing so helps me take the good with the bad. There will be times when not-so-great things occur in your life, but maintaining a positive attitude will allow you to get through them with a better outlook.

4. **I Pray.** Start each day off with prayer or meditation. Take a few minutes, to spend time with God. Check in with Him to make sure things are okay and acknowledge Him.

5. **I tackle my laundry every other day.** By the time the weekend comes around, I don't have seven or eight loads of clothes to wash. (If you have more than one child, then you understand what I'm talking about). Also, try folding your clothes as soon as you get them out of the dryer; if you're like me, you get them back to the house and instead of folding them immediately, they sit in the basket the entire week. If you decide to wait, you might find yourself living out of your laundry basket, and every morning, you'll be searching for something to wear.

7. **I make time for play.** When you have little ones, you pretty much work around their schedules, not the other way around. As I mentioned earlier, I have an eight-year-old son in third grade and a six-year-old daughter in first grade. Now that they're in school eight hours a day, I have time to work on my business with no interruptions. However, I recall when they were younger and home with me, and they would have temper tantrums. It was like they were trying to see who could cry the loudest. Kids are the only people on this earth who can scream and shout and get their way! Let me try that, and the only thing I'm going to get is, "LaTersa, you need to take care of that situation." During my me time, I grab a good inspirational book, or listen to one of my favorite songs. Beyoncè's "Get Me Bodied" or "Roar" by Katy Perry gets my adrenaline going.

8. **I cook dinner for one or two days.** When I prepare dinner, I try to make at least two days' worth. Now, don't get me wrong, I love cooking, but the key here is to make less work for yourself. If I'm cooking spaghetti, for example, I make enough for about three or four days; after the second day, the remainder goes into the freezer. Besides, spaghetti is better when it's left over.

9. **I put my kids on a schedule**. Once my kids are home from school, I sometimes let them play a little bit, then it's homework time. You might be thinking, *It should be homework first, then play*. And that is the usual routine, but on those days when my son wants to have a hissy fit, to keep from going insane or beating him like he stole something, I cater to his want. After homework time, we eat dinner, then it's bath time. By 8:30 P.M., all people eight and under are in bed with the audio bible on. Some-weekends, I let them fall asleep to their Veggie Tales movie.

10. **I have family time daily.** I try to incorporate it into my schedule every day. This is how I set it up: From 6:30 to 8:30 P.M., I spend time with our children, and from 8:30 to 10:00, I spend time with my husband. Now, I'm not perfect, so there are times when I'm like a zombie and have to call it a night early. But I always make sure I tell my family I love them before going to bed, and of course, I take care of hubby as well.

Chapter Nine: A Glimpse into LaTersa's World

Are you ready to go on an adventure with me? That's truly what a typical day at my house is like. My day starts at about 5:30 A.M. with prayer before my feet ever hit the floor. I get up 30 minutes earlier than everyone else on most days because I know I have to spend some time alone and in prayer before my little people get up. After I pray, I stand straight up and read my affirmations out loud so I can set the tone for my day.

Around six, I wake my little man and little girl up. They get washed up, dressed, ready for school, eat breakfast, then we're out the door to the bus stop.

Geesh, you mean to tell me I have the house all to myself for at least eight hours?! What shall I work on now? Should I do laundry, wash dishes or what? As I said earlier, doing household chores will not put money in your pockets. You'll have a clean house and no new clients, no money, and you might just be out of business. In my first year of marriage, I tried to be the perfect little wifey and perfect mommy. I wanted my house shiny and pristine with no toys on the floor. That mentality nearly drove me insane because when hubby got home, I was worn out from running behind my toddlers and cleaning up every little mess. At the rate I was going, I was headed for disaster.

I was also very resentful of my husband, because he would be so upbeat and jolly, and I was so dang tired. I was giving and giving and giving until it hit me that I must take care of me first.

Here's what I do now: Once I see the kids off to school, I spend one hour getting the kitchen cleaned, making sure the living room is at its best, and then I tidy up the bathroom, because those are the rooms our company uses; at the Blakely's house, no one is being entertained in the bedrooms. Most days, I make up my bed right after getting up, but for the days I don't get to it, I proudly close the door and do it after work hours.

After playing housekeeper for an hour, it's probably about eight, and it's time to get my work out on. I normally exercise for at least 30 minutes, then I juice and drink my lemon water, take a break to shower, and put on something cute. Just because I work from home doesn't mean I have to stay in my pajamas all day. In order for me to perform at my best, I have to also look my best. Putting on a cute outfit helps my creativity and puts my mind in a professional state.

It's now around nine, so it's off to working on my top three priorities I must complete for the day. I may not make it to the other things under the work section, but, I make it my business to do my most income-producing and client-attracting tasks first. Remember, an emergency could come up or the kids could get sick, so I want to make sure that my most pressing items are done. However, I don't panic if I don't get everything complete; there's always tomorrow. I am not super woman, and I only have two hands.

After making some phone calls and running some errands, it's now about 11:30. During this time, I try to avoid social media and texting so I can remain focused. I must admit, before I set a schedule, I spent a lot of unnecessary time on Facebook and Twitter, because I thought you needed to be on there to answer every question and see who liked your posts. I soon realized that doing this wasn't making me any money.

Here are a few tips to help you stay focused during your work hours:

- Set aside two to three hours to go hard on your daily business tasks.
- Use hootsuite.com to schedule your tweets and posts throughout the week.
- Stay away from all social media sites. Instead, use hyperalerts.no, a system that alerts you when someone responds to your Facebook fan page's updates.
- Drink plenty of water so you can stay energized (keep a bottle at your desk).
- Listen to motivational audios in case you get down or feel hopeless.

- Think positively; turn off those self-sabotaging thoughts and beliefs.
- Give yourself a pep talk when needed (not everybody will understand your new job).

Following these simple steps is a sure-fire way to have a productive work day.

Now, that I have completed my most pressing business tasks, it's now around noon. This is generally when I have my midday snack or lunch. Sometimes, I juice a big glass of veggies (carrots, cucumbers, spinach, beets) and fruits (pineapples, an apple, or raspberries). Then there are times when I want some meat, and I'll fix a honey turkey sandwich on wheat bread with chopped pineapples, apples and a handful of Lays® chips. Lunch is what I call my me time; it's when I unwind. I remove myself from my office and go into the living room (away from the laptop), because I want to enjoy my lunch, not think about work. I usually watch cooking shows or HGTV, or I read. During this time, I kick back, enjoy my lunch and reflect on my day thus far. This is also when I give myself pep talks if needed.

Now, it's about 12:30 or close to 1, so it's back to work for at least another hour to see what else I can accomplish before my babies are home from school. Around 3:45, I pick them up from the bus stop, then it's mommy and kiddos time. They get to tell me all about their day, what they learned, and how much fun they had. There may be times when they didn't have such great days, and that's when I kick my mommy skills up a notch or two. With Ishmael, you never know what story you're going to hear; it may go a little something like this: "Mommy, when I grow up, I'm going to open me up a McDonald's where they have rooms so if people get tired after they eat, they can just pay me to get one of my rooms." Did you catch that? My entrepreneurial spirit is rubbing off on him early. There are also days he comes home and says things like, "Mommy, I'm so tired; they didn't even let me take a nap."

After listening to all the stories of the day, they do their homework, then play so they can get tired. (Here's a little secret: Make sure you get them really, really tired and down right out of breath before bedtime). While I'm helping with homework, I'm starting dinner as well. This is where my multitasking skills are put to work. I'm the type of woman who loves to cook a fabulous meal, but I don't like to be in the kitchen all day. I love quick meals that are also healthy. You may be asking, "LaTersa, what are some quick meals I can cook for my family?"

Check out a few of my favorites:

- Hamburger Helper (4-Cheese Lasagna) with green beans and toast
- Tuna melts served on toasted bread
- Tilapia and french fries (I go crazy if I don't have fish at least twice per week.)

- Baked tilapia with spinach and lemons (Bake in the oven for 45 minutes on 400 degrees or until tender.)
- Turnip greens (Glory brand greens) with Mexican cornbread (You can buy the cornbread packages from Wal-Mart for 69 cents.)
- Grilled cheese sandwiches with green beans and carrot salad (Salad includes shredded carrots, pineapples and raisins.)

After dinner and homework, I let them play a little more, then it's off to take baths. Once that's complete, it's now around 5:30, time for the king of the castle to walk through the door any minute (if he's not working late). After greeting my boo, we have dinner together. On the days he works late, the kiddos and I eat together because I hate eating after eight; that's how all those unwanted guests (pounds) show up. After dinner, I normally let the kiddos choose a book to read for our nightly story time.

You may be wondering: What if my kids are out for the holidays and they're home with me all day? Glad you asked! Here are a few tips for having a productive work day while also being mom to your children:

- Create signals to let your kids know you're working and are not to be disturbed. My kids know that when I close and lock my office, they are not to knock, call my name or stick papers or toys under the door.
- Give them card games to play with like Uno.
- If they have a computer, let them play certain games. I allow my babies to play on pbskids.org, which is a learning tool, and my daughter likes to play dress up games, or watch cooking or Hello Kitty videos on YouTube.
- Play their favorite movie.
- If you can, take them to your parents' house for a few hours so you can get some work done.
- Bribe them. Yes ma'am, I do it all the time! For example, I'll tell them, "If you let mommy work for three hours straight, I'll take you to the movies or to the park."

After the kids are in bed, guess what time it is now? Yes, it's time to spend time with my husband — yippee. You have to carve out time to connect with your mate to keep things nice and spicy. I try to do something with him daily because as women, we can get so caught up in all of the other things and everybody else; if we're not careful, we'll start to neglect our spouses, and that's not good. Try to keep the line of communication open with him.

At this point in the evening, I look as high as a kite. If you could see how red my eyes are, you'd probably think I drank a whole bottle of tequila!

Finally, it's time to call it a night; but before I close my eyes, I say my prayers, read my affirmations, and make my to-do list for the next day. Then, I'm off to bed.
And there you have it; you've just spent an entire day with me!
So, tell me, what is a typical day like with you?

Chapter Ten: How To Balance Life as a Single Married Woman

You might be thinking, *What the heck is a single married woman?* A single married woman is a wife whose spouse is away from the house most of the time. Her husband could be serving active duty in the military, or he could be working for a company that requires him to travel often. This has the wife playing both roles in the home, not because she wants to, but because she has to. I am experiencing this right now, and I will be the first to say it is no easy task. Some days, I feel like pulling all of my hair out and screaming to the top of my lungs. My husband has been overseas for two years now, and when he first left, I cried myself to sleep because I missed him so much. I knew I'd have to play both roles and that everything was all on me. Before he left, we had a routine for accomplishing our day-to-day household chores and dealing with the kids. I had to create a new schedule that would work for my children and me.

If you feel like you're raising your kids alone, I feel your pain. This is the first time I've been away from my husband since we've been married, and I have learned a few things. Balance has a whole new meaning in my book.

So, let me share a few secrets on achieving balance while being a single parent temporarily:

1. **Change your schedule.** Since the responsibilities are on you now, rearrange your schedule. For example, if the kids are home for the summer, and you work from home, you can do most of your business tasks and household chores in the mornings, while they're sleeping. If you have younger children like I do, they usually sleep longer in the mornings. I use this time to work out, complete a few household chores, and make calls to clients.

2. **Get your parents involved.** I relocated to my home state when my husband left because I didn't want to be so far away with no help. Since we're at my parents' home, I have assistance with my children. On those days when I'm too tired for extracurricular activities, my parents usually take the kids for treats or to the park for a few hours to give me a break. If you don't live close to your family or you can't relocate, build relationships with your neighbors or even your church family; one of the church moms might be happy to babysit for a few hours.

3. **Have a date night with yourself.** This may sound cheesy, but you'd be amazed at how a day of nothing but fun and time away from the kids will

refresh and recharge your life. When you're doing everything alone, you tend to forget how to keep yourself together without losing your mind. Since my husband has been away, I've tried to make it my business to go out once a week for a shopping spree (even if it's just window shopping), dinner at my favorite restaurant, or a movie or two. I've even started going to jazz clubs because I've fallen in love with the serenity and sweet sound of jazz. Another great idea for date night with yourself is to take a class. A little unknown fact about me is I took a pole dancing class; I've always wanted to learn how to be sexy in my heels and for my husband. Don't hesitate to go out, and learn something new.

4. **Find age-appropriate activities.** My children love technology, so I allow them to play educational games on websites including pbskids.org. Not only do they learn new things, they're also engaged so I can take care of what I need to.

    a. **For older kids,** finding activities around the house can work to your advantage, especially if you are in business or just a working woman period. They can help you by doing the dishes, taking out the trash, doing laundry, or any other chores you might need help with.

    b. **For infants** – The baby's naptime is your time to shine, so use it to your advantage. When the house is quiet, you can operate better and much faster.

5. **Burn the midnight oil.** If you can't seem to get things done because your little ones require all of your attention, enjoy the peace and quiet after you put them down for the night. I will tell you this much: Some of my best work has been birthed during the midnight hours.

My Favorite Quotes for Mom Entrepreneurs & Moms

1) "There is no way to be a perfect mother, and a million ways to be a good one." – Jill Churchill

2) "You are more than enough, and everything that you need is already on the inside of you." – LaTersa Blakely

3) "A mother holds her children's hands for a while...their hearts forever." – Author Unknown

4) "Don't limit yourself. Many people limit themselves to what they think they can do. You can go as far as your mind lets you. What you believe, remember, you can achieve." – Mary Kay Ash

5) "When one door of happiness closes, another opens; but often we look so long at the closed door that we do not see the one which has opened for us." – Helen Keller

6) "I've learned that people will forget what you said, people will forget what you did, but people will never forget how you made them feel." – Maya Angelou

7) "Be thankful for what you have; you'll end up having more. If you concentrate on what you don't have, you will never, ever have enough." – Oprah Winfrey

8) "If you're able to be yourself, then you have no competition. All you have to do is get closer and closer to that essence." – Barbara Cook

9) "On your way up the success ladder, reach back and help someone else; so when you get to the top, you all can have a glass of wine instead of alone." – LaTersa Blakely

10) "Be careful how you treat people, you never know who you might need later on in life." – LaTersa Blakely

11) ""Shoot for the moon. Even if you miss, you'll land among the stars." – Les Brown

I want to hear about how you're balancing work and family, the new schedules you've set for yourself, and how it's working for you. Let's stay in contact: http://www.mommymavensrock.com

God bless you on your way to living a life of abundance in every area of your life!

My Book Recommendations for Moms & Mompreneurs

1) *Momproneur ~ Steps To Balance Work, Life & Love* by LaTersa Blakely

2) *The Power of a Praying Mom* by Stormie Omartian

3) *The Power of a Praying Wife* by Stormie Omartian

4) *The Secret of a Millionaire Mind* by T. Harv Eker

5) *Think and Grow Rich* by Napoleon Hill

6) *Knowing Your Value* by Mika Brzezinski

7) *From Entrepreneur to Infopreneur* by Stephanie Chandler

8) *Thou Shall Prosper* by Rabbi Daniel Lapin

9) *The Purpose-Driven Life* by Rick Warren

10) *I AM ENOUGH* by LaTersa Blakely

About the Author

LaTersa Blakely's life is a journey filled with business know-how and compassion. From her experiences, LaTersa reveals her purpose, and she is eager to share her purpose with all the women of the world.

Born in the Midwestern farming district of Holly Grove, Arkansas, LaTersa was a girl with ambition. She seized an opportunity to work in the agricultural industry through hands on learning — she literally got her hands dirty to get the job done! Years later, LaTersa earned a Bachelor's Degree in Agriculture Economics, a Master's Degree in Agriculture Business Management and a prominent position as a Soil Conservationist. Her duties included surveying the land, a task that would prepare her for digging into the roots of her clients' problems as a life coach.

The wife, mother of two, and woman of God decided to heed the calling on her life in 2010 after spending years in the corporate world. LaTersa found that through motivating other mothers, women entrepreneurs and the like, she needed to launch her own business. In 2011, the Mommy Maven was born.

Like everyone else, LaTersa understood that her work would need to include life balance. Unlike others, however, she managed to find that balance. In doing so, LaTersa penned articles for business blogs and e-zines, including Care2.com, a website committed to providing a better world through health and conservation news. Her way with words empowered her to pen her first book, "DIGG DEEP, Steps to Embrace Your Past and Step into Your Greatness," in 2012.

LaTersa's next work would serve as the blueprint for her life coaching business, now known as LaTersa Blakely Enterprises. "Mompreneur: Steps to Balance Work, Life and Love" was released in early 2013. The practical guide speaks to women of all walks of life, women who are ready to take back control of their lives. LaTersa now speaks for herself, literally: The mogul has been an invited guest speaker on several occasions, including Blogtalk Internet Radio. The "SistaSense Magazine"-featured mom entrepreneur and a two-time winner of Startup Nation's Leading Moms in Business has been hailed as motivational leader Les Brown's one to watch. He declared, "The world needs what (she) has to share."

Today, upon releasing her latest work in April 2014, "I AM ENOUGH" — a stop-the-pity-party manual for those seeking more in their lives — LaTersa spends time sharing through mentoring, hosting webinars and collaborating with women who hunger for clarity.

Get your FREE audio: 21 tips and tools for stay at home moms at http://www.mommymavensrock.com. Contact LaTersa on Facebook at http://www.facebook.com/theoriginalentrepreneur.

What people are saying about LaTersa & The Book

"This book is a great resource for any mom who is ready to start their own business, I seriously wish this book was around when I started my journey, I wanted to skip over the nuts and bolts and jump right into business and tap into my creative side, but LaTersa explains greatly in her book the importance of family, managing money, and running a successful business. This is an absolute must read right here!" –LaKeisha Hankins

"Moms: the Original Entrepreneur" is a primer for the mom who finds herself wanting to take advantage of all that life has to offer — and this includes making some extra money.

Raising a family is a full-time job in itself. "Moms: the Original Entrepreneur" gives the green light for those who dare to add a business venture into the daily mix.

An easy read, "Moms: the Original Entrepreneur" is a quick how-to for the busiest people on Earth, mothers who are looking to add the title of CEO to their resumes. LaTersa Blakely's own work — kingdom work — shines throughout "Moms: the Original Entrepreneur". Her explanation of a Proverbs 31 woman is spot on!

More on LaTersa's work: for those who find themselves still on fence about becoming a mompreneur, wait until you reach chapter nine!

LaTersa, the women's champ, does it again" – Tyjuana Wilson – Working mom

"LaTersa Blakely…. Wow, what can I say about this woman. When I think of the words I Am Enough and Balanced Woman, I think of this Mommy Expert. She is the person you call to gain her expertise at balancing how to run a successful home and business while raising children and loving it ALL, while not leaving out hubby! Her great sense of humor gives her a personality that everyone I know is drawn to like a moth to flame. If you are ever looking for someone to coach you in the area of Mompreneurship, she is the person to call."--Tamara G.

"Lady of Virtue. LaTersa is a woman who stands at the crossroad of life and brings others with her to their destiny. She is not a selfish woman that only looks out for herself but she unselfishly created a platform to show women that they are enough. God has blessed her with the skills and abilities to walk before others even through her own journey being the epitome of a helpmeet." –LaTanya H.

I want to take this time to say thank you so much for purchasing my book. If it has helped you in any way, I would love to hear from you! And if you have a group of moms or church members who would love to purchase this book in bulk quantities, you can contact us via email at info@latersablakely.com.

There is an order form on the following pages for your convenience.

As a friend of LaTersa Blakely and supporter for Moms ~ The Original Entrepreneur,
your network is entitled to <u>Discounted Prices</u> on the book:
I have also added an affiliate link that you can use; your associates
will receive a bookmark along with their book order.

<u>Moms ~ The Original Entrepreneur</u> (Retail Price $15.99) Affiliate Program link: http://www.e-junkie.com/lblakely/product/486815.php. Join our affiliate program and save!

<u>Moms: The Original Entrepreneur</u> Book (Retail Price $15.99)

<u>Qty</u>	<u>Your Prc/Bk</u>	<u>Total</u>	*We are interested in ordering_____ (Qty.) of this book.
22	$10.00	$239.80	*Print Name_____
42	$8.00	$366.24	*Contact Information_____
84	$7.00	$640.92	

Shipping & taxes are included in price, unless otherwise stated. All sales are final (no returns or refunds accepted).
To place an order, please call LaTersa Blakely at 256-603-5353 or email info@latersablakely.com.

<u>5 Reasons to Buy Books</u>

1. **REWARD** those who have helped your group by giving them a FREE autographed book.
2. **INCREASE ATTENDANCE** by advertising that the first _?_ people who attend the event will receive a FREE autographed book. Or, give away copies as **DOOR PRIZES**.
3. **BOOK SIGNING**. Advertising that LaTersa Blakely will be autographing books after the event will increase attendance.
4. **RECEIVE A LOWER PRICE** than what the books would sell for at the event.
5. **RAISE MONEY FOR YOUR GROUP** by selling the books at the event for the retail price. Each purchase through your network will also receive a bookmark.

***IDEA: If you're having a conference or including this as part of your membership bonuses, incorporate the cost per book into the registration fee, then have a book included in all registration packets.**

Journal

www.ingramcontent.com/pod-product-compliance
Lightning Source LLC
Chambersburg PA
CBHW031201090426
42736CB00009B/751